NATIONAL GEOGRAPHIC

Washington, D.C.

Gustav Blümchen

Have you been to Washington, D.C.?
It is the capital of the United States.
There are many famous places to visit
in Washington, D.C.

16.30
22 OCT
2002

This is the White House.
The President of the United States lives here.

The President works in the White House, too. The President works in this room, called the Oval Office.

This is the Capitol Building.
Congress meets here.

Members of Congress make laws for the country.
They meet in this room.

This is the Washington Monument.
It was built to honor George Washington, the first President of the United States.

The Washington Monument is the tallest building in Washington, D.C.
This is the view from the top of the Monument.

This is the Lincoln Memorial.
It was built to honor Abraham Lincoln.

Abraham Lincoln was President a long time ago.
This statue of him sits inside the Lincoln Memorial.

WASHINGTON
16.30
22 OCT
2002

This is the Air and Space Museum.
It is one of the many museums in Washington, D.C.

This airplane is on display in the museum.
You can learn about the history of flight here.

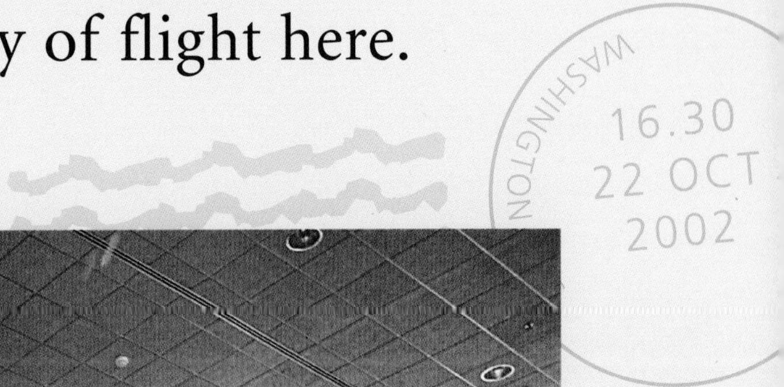

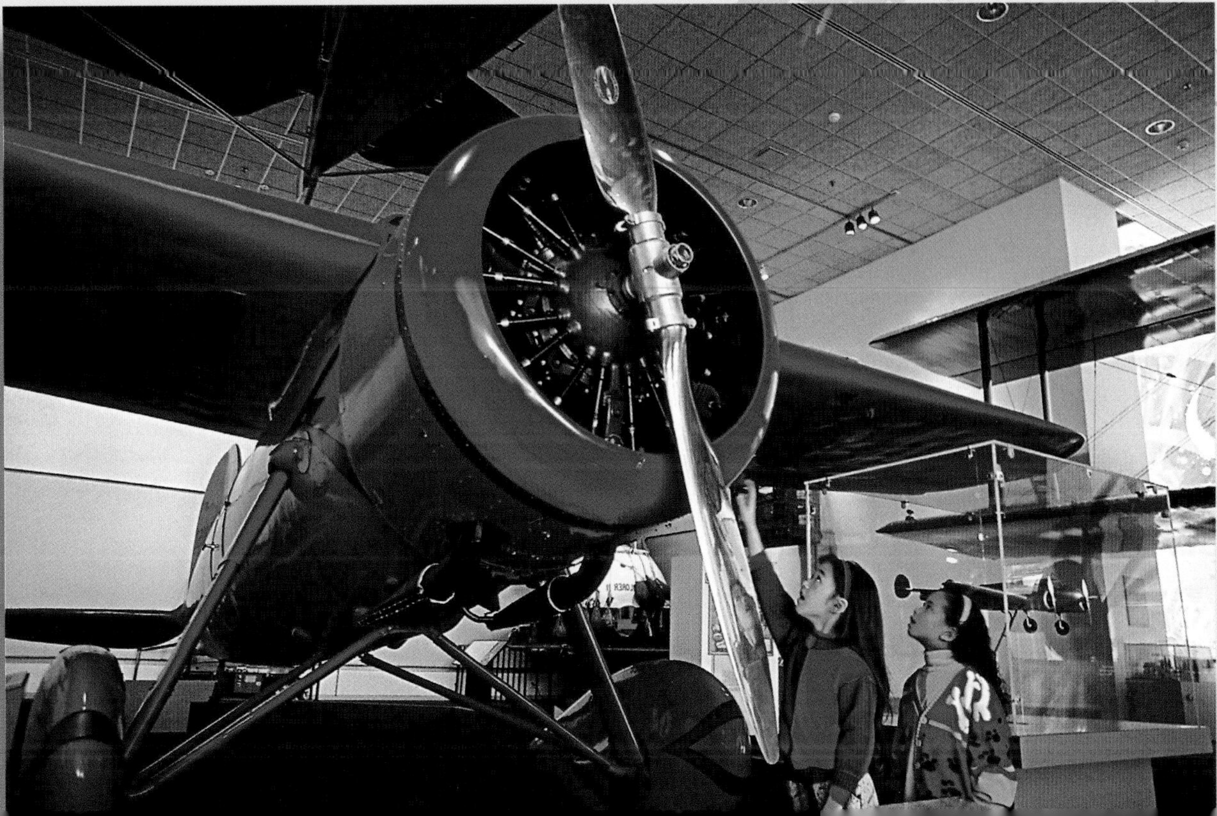

Which of these places would you like to visit?

White House

Capitol Building

Washington Monument

WASHINGTON, D
16.30
22 OCT
2002

Lincoln Memorial

Air and Space Museum

Index